C000021574

Expecting

Celebrating the Waiting & the Wonder

Nancy Moser

Harold Shaw Publishers

Wheaton, Illinois

To Mom and Dad

I knew I was loved.

Copyright © 1998 by Nancy Moser

All rights reserved. No part of this book may be reproduced or transmitted in any form or by any means, includng electronic or mechanical, photocopying, recording, or any information storage and retrieval system without written permission from Harold Shaw Publishers, Box 567, Wheaton, Illinois 60189. Printed in the United States of America.

All Scripture quotations, unless otherwise indicated, are taken from the HOLY BIBLE, NEW INTERNATIONAL VERSION ®. NIV ®. Copyright © 1973, 1978, 1984 International Bible Society. Used by permission of Zondervan Publishing House. All rights reserved.
    The "NIV" and "New International Version" trademarks are registered in the United States Patent and Trademark Office by International Bible Society. Use of either trademark requires permission of International Bible Society.
    Scripture quotations marked NLT are taken from the *Holy Bible, New Living Translation*, copyright © 1996 Tyndale House Publishers, Inc., Wheaton, Illinois 60189. All rights reserved.

ISBN 087788-610-5

Library of Congress Cataloging-In-Publication Data

Moser, Nancy.
    Expecting : a celebration of waiting and wonder / by Nancy Moser.
        p.   cm.
    ISBN 0-87788-610-5
    1. Pregnancy–Humor.   2. Childbirth–Humor.   3. Motherhood–Humor.   I. Title.
    RG556.M67 1998
    618.2'4—dc21
                                                                                98-27614
                                                                                CIP

Cover and inside design by David LaPlaca

02 01 00 99 98

10 9 8 7 6 5 4 3 2 1

What's Inside

PART 1
Ready, Set, Go! 7

PART 2
Getting Your Feet Wet without Drowning .25

PART 3
Practice Makes (Almost) Perfect 43

PART 4
Pulling It Off 63

PART 1

Ready, Set, Go!

Make Me a Mom!

If you already have something, you don't need to hope for it. But if we look forward to something we don't have yet, we must wait patiently and confidently.
—*Romans 8:24-25 (NLT)*

How many times did you *hope* to be pregnant before you actually *became* pregnant? Hope is a mysterious thing. And hoping to be pregnant kindles a force of nature more powerful than the atom bomb. There is nothing more inspiring or more annoying than a woman firing up her maternal instincts. Ready or not . . . make me a mom.

Being pregnant is psychological as well as physical. However, just as the body can often fool us, so can the mind. I *knew* I was pregnant many times when I wasn't. Just as you can mentally make yourself sick, I attempted the mental gymnastics to *think* myself pregnant. If I had been successful, I surely would have won a gold medal for my mindsprings.

And just imagine how overpopulated the world would be if we got pregnant every time we had the notion. Why, I would have been with child every time I cooed over someone else's baby in the mall. Good thing God makes it a bit more difficult.

I got pregnant with Emily, my first, before I had ever heard of in-home pregnancy tests. I wasn't sure just how the discovery system worked. So I asked the doctor who had delivered *me*. I was told to bring in an early-morning urine sample and they'd test it. How, why or with what I didn't know, but as this was only one of a thousand things in life I didn't understand (such as: Why do fingernails have moons? and why are tomatoes classified as fruit?), I did as I was told.

The trouble was, I had to be at work at eight and the doctor's office didn't open until nine. How was Exhibit A supposed to get to the doctor's office? I did what any naive twenty-two-year-old would do. I left it in a sack by the outer door of the office. If crime were high in Nebraska I might never have known I was expecting, and some wayward thief would have found himself very confused.

The waiting was hard; the wondering was worse. But through it all I felt awe as the spark of hope became the spark of life. As the apostle Paul said, anyone can hope for what she can see, but to hope for the unseen, for a new life, something that does not exist until God decides it's time . . . that's hope. And faith.

Maybe hope isn't so mysterious after all. Maybe hope for life *is* life.

 ## Wacky Wives' Wisdom:

Mistletoe increases fertility.
   (Well, it does start with a kiss. . . .)

Why "Planned" and "Parenthood" Don't Mix

But those who hope in the Lord will renew their
strength. They will soar on wings like eagles; they will
run and not grow weary, they will walk and not be faint.
—*Isaiah 40:31*

When it came to scheduling the birthdates of our children, we thought we were in control. Mark and I always wanted to have kids. It wasn't a question of if, but when. Our main concern was that the pregnancy fit into *our* schedule.

In regard to the biggies of life—jobs, homes, and family—Mark and I have never been keen on surprises. Surprise us with a birthday cake, an unexpected hour of free time, or tickets to a movie, and we're thrilled, but surprise us with something that is either life-changing or inconvenient, and we'll pass. Next category, please.

Yet as much as we thought we had control of the timing of my pregnancies, we didn't. God did. Deep down we knew his timing was perfect, but we still didn't appreciate how he chose to test us. Pregnancy shows a wanton disregard for day-planners.

Our first lesson in God's timing started in college. Mark and I got married with two years of architecture school left. Following *our* schedule, we planned to get pregnant immediately after graduation.

It didn't work that way.

A few years later, when we decided it was time to have our second child, I was heavily involved in community theater, and tryouts for the spring musical were usually in early March. I wanted to have the baby prior to that so I could sing and dance my way through *Mame*.

It didn't work that way.

And when we decided to have a third child, we wanted to have her before March 13 when Mark and I were going to London on a business trip.

It *barely* worked that way. I had Laurel on March 2. We did go on the trip, which is another story, mostly having to do with intestinal fortitude and outright stupidity.

In the twenty years that have passed since the first rabbit died, we've discovered that schedules are for trains and planes—and even those schedules are rarely on the mark. If a DC-10 can be flexible, so can we.

The point is, good things are worth the wait. The seeds of patience and endurance are planted in the waiting. Character ripens with the disappointment, and gratitude and praise bloom when we are finally rewarded with the words, "You're going to have a baby."

Remember those attributes: patience, endurance, character, gratitude, and praise. You will visit them again. And again. According to God's schedule, not necessarily yours. And that is very, very good.

Wacky Wives' Wisdom:

If you can walk around the block with your mouth full of water you will have a baby within a year.

(Maybe if you can add a stirring rendition of "Dixie," you'll have twins.)

Milking the Moment

Many, O Lord my God, are the wonders you have done.
The things you planned for us no one can recount to
you; were I to speak and tell of them, they would be too
many to declare.
—*Psalm 40:5*

There are hundreds of creative ways to tell your husband you're pregnant, but when I was pregnant with baby #1, Emily, I didn't even think of being creative. I said the words, there was global rejoicing, and that was that. But by the time I was pregnant with babies #2 and #3, I was up for a little showmanship. Truth was, I wanted to milk the moment.

For Carson (baby #2) I decided to have a birthday party (get it? *birth*-day party?). I baked a cake, hung balloons from the chandelier, and set the table with our best china. Mark's first reaction was perfect: "What's this?"

"It's a birthday party."

"Who's it for?"

"The baby."

"What baby?"

I couldn't have scripted it better.

For Laurel (baby #3), I created handmade greeting cards that said, "Happy Father's Day," "Happy Brother's Day," and "Happy Sister's Day" on the front. Inside was a picture of an infant and the words "Love, Baby."

Mark was happy and the kids were curious. When told the baby was in my abdomen and was very, very small, six-year-old Emily asked, "Is it the size of a raisin?" Three-year-old Carson asked, "Is it as big as a spider in my sandbox?" If you study these reactions you will gain keen insight into my children's interests, if not their characters.

My reaction to my announcement was always the same. I cried. I'd like to blame it on hormones, but I can't. I am a crier. I cry at "Bonanza" reruns, coffee commercials, and any rendition of the "Hallelujah Chorus." I cried because I was happy, scared, overwhelmed, and awed.

But I figure it's allowed. After all, crying is a completely appropriate reaction to a miracle. And if we want to milk our little moment—I think we're entitled. After all, we've got about forty weeks of waiting ahead of us.

Wacky Wives' Wisdom:

You can get pregnant by swimming in a coed pool.
   (*You* can *also get water up your nose, pruned skin, and green hair.*)

15

A Twinkie to Your Health

Give me neither poverty nor riches, but give me only my
daily bread.
—*Proverbs 30:8*

If our children only knew what we sacrificed to bring them into the world. They say that, left to their own devices, children will eat the healthy food that their bodies need. However, I know from hard experience that left to her own devices, an *adult* will *not* eat healthy food. An adult will eat junk food. One of the questions I want God to answer is why things that are creamy and sweet set off our tastebuds in ways broccoli and cantaloupe don't.

But as much as I might have loved bad stuff, the presence of an unborn child who was forced to eat what I ate—and grow and thrive on that diet—made me reassess my choices. Such weighty responsibility.

I don't like restrictions. There was a short moment, when the doctor said "no caffeine" and "no artificial sweetener," that I considered mutiny. But the threat of insurrection passed and I nodded, resolved to be a good mother, no matter what the sacrifice. Good-bye, four cups of coffee. *Adieu,* diet drinks. Farewell, my dearest chocolate. If our kids only knew.

Modern medical science is an amazing blessing—but also terribly unfair. When our mothers were pregnant with us, who knew that caffeine was a no-no? Past generations of mothers drank coffee, ate chocolate, smoked cigarettes, and even drank alcohol. And look at us. We turned out okay. Mostly.

Nowadays, we *know* more about how to produce a healthy baby; therefore, we need to *do* more. Bring out the apples, the milk, the lean meats. Banish the Ding Dongs, Doritos, and anything where the grease rubs off on a napkin.

Maybe eating right will be good for *me*. Maybe the presence of my baby will make me change my bad habits forever.

Nah. I believe God put chocolate chip cookies and French fries on this earth for us to enjoy—in moderation (ah, the curse of moderation). But I'll work on it. Perhaps after the baby's born I'll celebrate with a Twinkie and . . . a glass of skim milk.

God will be so proud.

 ## Wacky Wives' Wisdom:

Late-night snacking gives you nightmares.
  (*I'll risk it.*)

Bathrooms and Bedtimes

When your endurance is fully developed, you will be
strong in character and ready for anything.
—*James 1:4 (NLT)*

My eyes open to darkness. My mind does a quick body search to decipher the reason I've awakened. It pinpoints my lower abdomen.

No! Not again!

I stagger out of bed. My feet fall into the path that is being worn in the carpet between the bed and the bathroom. They shuffle steadily along, the radar in my toes taking over since my eyes remain shut. I do my duty and return to bed.

It's evening. I'm curled on the couch, mimicking the fetal position of my baby. The opening credits of my favorite television show begin. I hear the theme music. I hear the clock strike eight. I fall asleep until Mark wakes me at ten so I can transfer my traitorous body into a real bed. But first, I take a short detour to the bathroom.

I'd like to know one thing: *What's going on?*

Although I longed to have this baby, I think it is totally unfair that I didn't get to vote on whether I wanted to run out of steam before sundown or become a stockholder in Charmin by default. I eventually stopped going to all concerts and sporting events and let someone else use my ticket because I ended up snoozing in my seat, or I was out of my seat, standing in line at the women's restroom (which never had enough stalls).

And on car trips? It got to the point where Mark pulled into every rest stop as if a giant magnet grabbed hold of the front bumper.

It helped to remember that my inconvenience was for a good cause. In a few months I'd be holding a snuggly baby in my arms and I'd forget about the numerous trips to the bathroom and the feeling of exhaustion.

Who was I trying to kid? It would never be over. There would be years of midnight runs to the bathroom with sick kids. My social life would be permanently altered. There would be weariness and worry and no privacy. So I had better get used to it and feel blessed by it—*all* of it.

By the way, I've figured out why there are longer lines in women's restrooms than in men's: men don't get pregnant. Ah, the price of motherhood!

Wacky Wives' Wisdom:

Don't sleep in a room with plants. At night they will use up the air and asphyxiate you.

(I knew there was a reason I kill all my houseplants. It's them or me.)

From "Me" to "We"

Do not forget to do good and to share with others,
for with such sacrifices God is pleased.
—*Hebrews 13:16*

I'm greedy. I want it all. I want a nice figure, time alone with my husband, freedom to do what I want, when I want to do it. And I want a baby.

Trouble is, having a baby wipes out my nice figure; threatens to make our couple time, triple time; and ties me to a schedule of "eats, sleeps, and wets" having nothing to do with when *I* feel like handling any eating, sleeping, or wetting.

Suddenly the world no longer revolves around me. Or even thee, dear husband—but *we*, as in "we three." The new king or queen of our house will be a dictator, putting to shame all totalitarian tyrants across the globe. When the baby cries, we'll come running, eager to say, "What is your wish, O lofty master?" And the baby won't even be polite enough to tell us. We'll have to guess, checking for pins, wet tushies, too-hots or too-colds, empty tummies, and even bored psyches. And if—if—we guess correctly, our tiny tyrant will grace us with a smile or a coo. And we'll fall all over ourselves for that bit of royal favor.

It's hard to learn a new role. I've spent all of my life being a daughter, some of my life being a wife, and I'm just beginning to figure out what that means. And now I have to learn this new job? Sure, I pursued the position, but is it so wrong to question the sacrifices and compromises that come with the job description?

Yes, it is.

I'll say it again: Children are a blessing from God. *Having* children is a blessing from God. We can either tolerate the experience or revel in it.

The psalmist instructs, "Offer right sacrifices and trust in the Lord" (4:5). Some sacrifice, a lot of trust. Not a bad formula for succeeding at this most important of all jobs.

Wacky Wives' Wisdom:

Cold hands, warm heart.
  (*Mittens can take care of one, but the other takes a little more work.*)

How Old Is a "Mabel"?
...and other name games

A good name is more desirable than great riches;
to be esteemed is better than silver or gold.
—*Proverbs 22:1*

W hat's in a name?" wondered the fair Juliet. "That which we call a rose by
any other name would smell as sweet."

Juliet was very naive. I know for a fact that if a rose were called "aardvark" its
smell would be tainted by its name. Giving your love a dozen aardvarks might take
on new symbolism. And "Aardvarks are red, violets are blue" just doesn't sing.

So what is in a name?

Plenty. Every prejudice you've ever held; every stereotype, bias, and image true
and imagined. Remember that bully who pulled your hair? No child of yours is
going to be named after him. Or your aunt who has a tendency to whine. Or the
crooked politician. Or the immoral movie star.

Second only to your decision to have a child is the monumental task of choosing what to call the little darling. There are many factors:

- **Frequency Forecast:** When I was in elementary school there were five Nancys in my class. How I envied my friends who were named Priscilla, Michaela, and Greta—unique, interesting names. Choosing a name is similar to getting a good grade in school: originality will always earn extra credit points. But don't get carried away. Don't doom your child to spelling her name aloud for the rest of her life.

- **Decade Definers:** How old is a Mabel? A Frank? A Debbie? An Amber? A Nancy, for that matter? Don't date your child. Of course there might be a rare case when decade-definers would be appropriate: How about Millennium ("Mill" for short)?

- **Cutesy Caution:** Buffy and Muffy will be doomed to be ditzy East Coast socialites forever—even if they live in Seattle. Stone and Rock will get a complex if their physiques don't live up to their names. Save cutesy for kittens, teddy bears, and advertising jingles.

- **Nix the Nicknames:** We purposely picked names that were difficult to shorten—Emily, Carson, and Laurel. Is your Robert going to be called Bob or Bobby or Rob or Robby? Remember that the Christopher you cherish may become Chris; the Elizabeth that sounds so elegant might become the more lowly Liz.

The whole name game is confounding—but take heart. Choosing the wrong name won't doom your child's potential (though it may test it a bit). Nor does the right name guarantee perfection. In fact, in spite of all your careful planning, your child might grow up and change his name to Elvis or Madonna. The important thing is to do your best with a spirit of wisdom and love, and then raise your child to live up to her or his name—whatever it is.

Wacky Wives' Wisdom:

Deep thinking makes you thin.
(I must have shallow thoughts.)

PART 2

Getting Your Feet Wet without Drowning

Lookin' Good!

Your beauty . . . should be that of your inner self, the
unfading beauty of a gentle and quiet spirit, which is of
great worth in God's sight.
—*1 Peter 3:3-4*

Remember Yankee Doodle, who played the fashion game by sticking a feather
in his hat? They called him "macaroni"—in those days, a term of admiration.
When I, as a pregnant lady, tried to look chic, they probably called me "rigatoni"
behind my back—in other words, twisted. Twisted for thinking I could possibly stay
in style.

Maternity clothes *have* improved in recent years. When I was first pregnant
back in 1977, most maternity tops were full of bows and Peter Pan collars, making
you look like a naughty six-year-old. Finding clothes that looked businesslike and
sophisticated was nearly impossible—of course, considering that polyester doubleknit was the fabric of choice back then, it may have been understandable. *No
one* ever looked businesslike in aqua doubleknit. Nineteen seventy-seven was also
the year it became popular to wear a shirt that had an arrow pointing toward your

belly with the caption "BABY" emblazoned above—just in case anyone had any doubt.

As the years passed and I had babies #2 and #3, there seemed to be a maternity revolution. It was as if the clothing designers of the world discovered that style and pregnancy could be compatible. (Of course, the banishment of doubleknit into leisure-suit heaven was instrumental in this revelation.) Suddenly, there were maternity suits and dresses without bows at the neck. There were tailored pants and coats and skirts and even jeans. It was as if after centuries of trying to cover up the pregnant condition, the garment industry decided to enhance it.

It was time for the world to acknowledge what we women already knew: There is nobody more "macaroni" than a pregnant lady—with or without a feather.

Wacky Wives' Wisdom:

Don't use a sewing machine or the vibrations will wrap the umbilical cord around the baby's neck.

(I suppose this means roller coasters are out?)

Moving Moments

"I prayed for this child, and the Lord has granted me
what I asked of him."
—*1 Samuel 1:27*

You are sitting on the couch, watching a rerun of "Leave It to Beaver," thinking how simple life was back then. The June Cleavers of the world stayed at home and wore high heels and pearl earrings while making dinner. They always kept a cookie jar filled with oatmeal cookies fresh from the oven—cookies that weren't sliced from a roll of dough. You're sitting there, watching Ward, in a suit and tie, give June a polite peck on the cheek. You wonder: *Was life really like that back then? That simple? That—*

Then you feel a flutter in your midsection. Your hand covers the spot protectively. You hold your breath, not wanting to scare the flutter away.

"What's wrong—"

You stop your husband's question with a hand. *No! No sounds! Don't move. Don't even blink.*

Is it indigestion? Is it hunger rumbling? Is it—

There it is again! A soft little thump from the inside out. A gentle nudge, a touch announcing this new existence: *It's your baby! It's alive! It's real!*

You grab onto your husband's hand and pull it to your abdomen. "There! Did you feel it?"

He shakes his head. Wistfully, you realize the baby's Morse code is too delicate for outside hands to feel. You feel privileged that you have been chosen to savor this unique communication between mother and child.

As the weeks pass, your vocabulary expands as you and baby learn each other's nonverbal language. You tell each other good morning and good night. You speak in soothing tones and the baby reacts to your gentle protection.

Eventually, as baby's feet and elbows grow, your husband is let in on the conversations. He feels the kick and the nudge and can even watch the movement across your belly as the baby gets comfortable. With your hand leading his hand to the spot where you both can feel your child, you become a family months before you see each other, months before you can touch skin to skin.

God is very wise. For in those months of waiting, he gives us a chance to get to know each other. He gives us a chance to learn how to be a family—with or without the pearls and cookie jars.

Wacky Wives' Wisdom:

A drop of mother's milk protects a newborn baby's eyes.
    (*No wonder they can't focus.*)

The Maypole Lesson

Love is patient and kind. . . .
—1 Corinthians 13:4 (NLT)

You start noticing other people's kids when you get pregnant. You also notice how other people treat their kids. It happened to me one Sunday in church. . . .

I smiled at the four-year-old girl sitting in the pew in front of me. She was dressed in the quintessential Sunday attire: a pastel dress with a crisp white collar, lace-edged anklets, and patent-leather shoes. She'd turned around to peek at us. We flirted a bit, and then I put a finger to my lips and pointed at the pastor, showing her it was time to be still.

She turned around like a good girl. For a little while.

The next time she caught my attention, she had removed one shoe and one sock . . . and she was twirling the sock on her big toe. I wondered how long it would take her mother to notice.

Her mother grabbed the sock and tried to put it on the bare foot, which was akin to putting a sock on an eel. Especially when the eel slithered away into the side aisle, just out of her mother's reach.

The mother made a halfhearted grab toward the little girl, but her options were limited in the sanctity of the church. And the little girl knew it. As her mother chose the "it's best to ignore her" route, ostensibly turning her attention to the sermon, the girl sneaked her mother's mammoth shoulder bag from under the pew and lugged it out to her showcase in the aisle. There she put the strap on her shoulder, leaving the weight of the bag to act as a pivot. She proceeded to march around the bag, one shoe on, one shoe off, like a Maypole devotee gone astray.

I watched this little drama, wondering: Would she get a smack on the fanny? Would she get yanked away to the narthex for a proper scolding?

The mother reddened and put a hand to her mouth, trying to hide a laugh. After a few rotations of the Maypole, the child heeded her mother's patting of the pew and sat down, accepted into the sanctuary of her mother's arm. A stern finger was pointed at her nose and an extra squeeze beneath the arm indicated she had better stay put. And she did.

I was amazed. My first reaction to the child's blatant (but cute) misbehavior had been to chastise and gain control. Sure, I'd have made a scene, but the other parents in the congregation would have understood that strict discipline was essential in order for the child to know who was boss. And yet I had just witnessed another way, a calmer way. Had the child won the battle of control? Maybe. But maybe it didn't matter. What had surfaced from the exchange between mother and child was not a battle at all, but a mutual exchange of love. Fun love. Tolerant love. And forgiving love.

Would I get it right with my own child? Would I be a good parent who would know when to allow some fun, when to be tolerant, and when to be tough? Would I have a heart big enough to always forgive?

I bowed my head and prayed that *I'd* be forgiven—for all the mistakes I'd make in future years with my own children.

The little girl sneaked another smile my way as if she understood—and approved of my effort.

 ## Wacky Wives' Wisdom:

Saying "God bless you" when someone sneezes can stop them from sneezing again.

(Saying "I forgive you" when someone does wrong is always right. For both parties.)

Chartreuse Caboose

Intelligent people are always open to new ideas. In fact,
they look for them.
—*Proverbs 18:15 (NLT)*

One reason I wanted to have children was so I would have another room to decorate—my way. No masculine plaids or stripes. No navy, burgundy, or gray. Neat colors like mint green, sunflower yellow, sky blue, and cotton candy pink.

I would like to report that there are 2,844,571 paint colors in the world—and I have seen them all. My mind grew numb as I pondered the decorating possibilities of Azure Morning, Coca-latte, and Capricorn Canyon. (Who names these colors, anyway? What sane person can come up with new names for the thirty-seven shades of white in their line?)

So when I first said I wanted to paint the walls of the baby's room Chartreuse Caboose, Mark thought I'd gone batty. "What color's that?" he asked.

I got out the sample and showed him a one-by-two-inch piece. "Chartreuse."

"What color's that?"

"Green."

"Why don't they just say that?"

"I think it's against the rules," I said.

"So what color's Caboose?"

"No color," I tried to explain. "It's the end car of a train, the last car—"

"I know that. But I thought cabooses were red?"

"They are, but in this case . . ." I sank into a chair, my stomach feeling a bit chartreuse under the circumstances.

Mark had mercy on me and didn't make me explain the unexplainable. "But what if it's a boy?" he asked.

"Boys like green, don't they? Grass green? Or maybe grass-stain green?"

He cocked his head, thinking. "Can you find one called Grass Green?"

"I think that would be too dark," I said. Also too logical and too normal. I flicked the sample against my hand, trying to think of a way to get my way. Then I had an idea. "Boys like trains, don't they?"

"Sure. At least I always did."

"A caboose is on a train . . ." I said, leaving him to get the connection.

"Red cabooses. Not green ones."

"Is there a law that says cabooses can't be green?"

"Of course not."

"Then they can be any color they want to be?" I knew I was reaching but I *really* liked this color.

"I suppose *if* a caboose had an opinion on the matter, it could be pink if it wanted to be," he replied with a sigh.

"Hmm," I said, pretending to ponder. "Pink. We could go pink. A dainty rose, maybe a blush—"

"Green is fine," he said, moving to leave the room and be away from this torture.

"Even Chartreuse Caboose?"

He turned in the doorway and gave me one of his looks. "I know what you just did," he said.

I put a hand to my chest, feigning innocence. "Me? What did—"

He raised a hand, stopping me. "You owe me."

I understood completely. "I owe you and love you," I said.

He left the room, shaking his head in that way husbands do when they realize they've lost. I went to the paint store. Some victories are very sweet.

 ## Wacky Wives' Wisdom:

If you are argumentative before birth your baby will be fussy.
(Who are you calling argumentative?)

Everyone's an Expert!

"What advice you have offered to one without wisdom!
And what great insight you have displayed!"
—Job 26:3

It's a fact: everyone knows everything about having babies. Especially yours.
In *Gone with the Wind* Prissy whined, "I don't know nothin' 'bout birthin' babies." If that's true, she's the only one.

At no time in my life did I come across so many experts. Bank tellers, cashiers, the people standing behind me in line at the grocery store. Everyone knew the best, the most perfect way to be pregnant and give birth—or—if they had a "unique" experience in doing so, they feel compelled to tell me about it in detail.

"I only gained twelve pounds when I was pregnant. I didn't have to wear maternity clothes until the eighth month."

"I gained eighty-five pounds and my husband said he didn't mind that I've never lost the last forty of it."

And then comes the question: "How much have *you* gained?"

As you move along in your pregnancy, the stories start turning toward the actual birth. You will hear horror stories of five days in labor, along with various versions of having the baby on the front lawn of the hospital. (Everyone seems to know someone this happened to.)

And everyone's a critic. When they see you buying strawberries they will warn you that eating strawberries will give your baby a strawberry birthmark. If you've slipped in a candy bar, they will remind you that chocolate contains caffeine.

Your first reaction is to get revenge by remarking that it might be wise if they chose sherbet instead of chocolate-chocolate chip ice cream, considering they look as pregnant as you do. But you restrain yourself; you smile and nod and act as if you care that they care.

And that's why you can't jump all over them: they *care*. The whole world cares that you are pregnant and they want to help. It's as if your baby belongs to the larger community that is humankind. And they all want your baby to be healthy and happy.

So take the bits of advice offered by the world. Accept them in the spirit they are given—of love.

Wacky Wives' Wisdom:

Don't let your baby wear shoes until he stands or they will hurt his feet. *Alternative wisdom:* Make sure your baby wears shoes from birth so his feet will grow strong.

(Do you have an opinion about socks?)

God's Voice, Mom's Intuition

Faith is being sure of what we hope for
and certain of what we do not see.
—*Hebrews 11:1*

I did not know my children's genders before they were born. Although nowadays it seems everyone but the mailman knows, back in 1978, 1981, and 1985 it was not an option I was ever given. I didn't know because the doctor didn't know. God kept his secret well.

But just because I didn't know didn't mean that I didn't *know*.

I knew. Three times I knew the sex of our children before they were born. Who needs technology? Who needs doctors? I had something far more powerful—mother's intuition.

When I was pregnant with Emily, I always thought of her as a girl. Same with Laurel. And middle child Carson? My thoughts of him were always masculine. This sense extended to the names we picked out. With the two girls we had definite female names ready while the boys' names remained sketchy. With Carson, just the opposite occurred.

This mother's intuition is worth study. Yet by the time scientists could dissect its origins and power, they'd give credit to some molecule located in the left quadrant of our pituitary gland or some other scientific mumbo-jumbo. They would ruin the essence of this God-given intuition.

Truth is, I don't want to know why I felt this way. Or how. I enjoyed feeling the special wisdom my intuition afforded. It was as if my babies were already communicating with me, letting me know who they were. It was as if God were communicating with me, giving me a special sense of the gifts that were to come.

I regret that I didn't trust my distinct boy-girl feelings. I still hedged my bets on the colors of the babies' rooms and their clothes, choosing the neutrals of babyhood, the greens and oranges and yellows, instead of declaring my faith with baby blue and pink.

God speaks to us through our intuition, giving us glorious hints about his miracles. If only we had the kind of faith that took chances. *That* would be a true miracle.

 ## Wacky Wives' Wisdom:

What you eat can determine the sex of your baby.
  (*I wonder what malted milk balls and nachos determine?*)

PART 3

Practice Makes (Almost) Perfect

Who's That You're Talking To?

"When you came in and greeted me, my baby jumped for joy the instant I heard your voice!"
—*Luke 1:44 (NLT)*

We took birthing classes at a local hospital. One of the things I learned from the classes was how to breathe—something I'd always considered I had down pat. Before we went home each week, I dragged Mark on a detour to the hospital nursery. There we would look at the new babies and sigh with impatience.

Soon. Very soon.

It was in front of that nursery window that I experienced a strange phenomenon: "cuddle ache." It was a condition that was part physical, part emotional. I wanted—needed—to hold a baby in my arms. I wanted to hold *my* baby in *my* arms.

Mark would nod politely when I'd try to explain this yearning, but he didn't get it. Although he was excited about having a baby on the way, it became clear that cuddle ache was a distinctly female condition, probably stemming from the fact that we lived with the baby so close—and yet so far from our willing arms.

Since I couldn't hold my baby, I sang to it (him, her). Read to it. Talked to it. I usually did this in private as some conversations are meant just for two. Yet it was inevitable that Mark would overhear. . . .

The first time it happened was while I was making chocolate chip cookies. I'd already done all the mixing and was in the process of dropping the dough onto the cookie sheets. Because I like all the cookies to be the same size, I was rolling them into balls.

"See?" I said to Baby. "If you put a little water on your hands the dough won't stick. I like to put no more than sixteen cookies on each—"

"Who are you talking to?"

I turned to see Mark in the kitchen doorway. I lifted my chin in defiance and rescued a squished cookie from between my palms. "You scared us."

Mark's eyebrows raised. "Us?"

Maybe I'd gone too far. "Me. You scared me."

"I sincerely hope you're practicing to be the next Julia Child; telling your television audience how to cook." He paused. "The alternative is too frightening."

I tossed my hair. "I'm teaching our baby how to make great chocolate chip cookies."

"Ah."

His "Ah" was worth a thousand words. "Don't ah me," I said. "The baby calms when it hears my voice."

"What if he or she has questions?"

I hesitated. "It doesn't. Our child is very smart for its age."

"But its mother's sanity is questionable." He hooked his finger through the cookie dough and left the room. "Carry on, you two."

I patted my abdomen. "There, there," I said. "You like it when I talk to you, don't you?"

The baby kicked. I smiled and continued with the cooking lesson. "The cookies seem to come out better when I only put one pan in the oven. It takes more time but the results are worth it."

Exactly. Bonding with my children before they were born took more time—but the results were worth it.

Wacky Wives' Wisdom:

Babies don't like loud music.
    (*Wanna bet? My children used to jive to Barry Manilow's* "Copacabana"—*in utero and out.*)

Coveting Duckies

They will celebrate your abundant goodness and joyfully
sing of your righteousness.
—*Psalm 145:7*

A baby shower makes it tough to obey the tenth commandment: "Thou shalt not covet."

How can you not covet those terry cloth sleepers that simply beg for a baby squirming within their seams? Or booties as big as your thumb? Or blankets you'd like to permanently borrow for yourself?

Baby showers are full of oohs and aahs—much more so than wedding showers, as it is hard to ooh and ahh over frying pans and monogrammed towels. It is impossible not to sigh at presents that are covered with duckies and bunnies.

Besides supplying the mother-to-be with goodies, baby showers serve two other purposes: they give grandmas-to-be a chance to overindulge, and they help the waiting go a little easier for the mama. The Bible says, "With the Lord a day is like a thousand years, and a thousand years are like a day" (2 Pet. 3:8). To a pregnant woman nine months is like a million. So while we wait forever, baby showers provide us with a rest stop, complete with a restroom, refreshments, and recreation.

Recreation . . . as in shower games. I hate shower games, even though I am very good at them. Yet, Guess the Advertiser, Word Scramble, and Memory Tray are minor annoyances we have to endure, annoyances that come with prizes! Give me the opportunity to win a prize, and my competitive nature leaps forward. So what if the prize is a rattle shaped like a safety pin? It's a *prize*.

As you see, showers are a mixed blessing. Gifts, laughter, and fruit "pizza" mix with shower games, too-sweet punch, and envy. But above all, baby showers make us covet the miracle. If it's our baby shower, we wallow in the fact that it's our turn. If we are merely a guest, the shower makes us remember our own moment in the sun, or look to the future with wistful anticipation and wonder.

Always, there is wonder: "Many, O Lord my God, are the wonders you have done. The things you planned for us no one can recount to you; were I to speak and tell of them, they would be too many to declare" (Ps. 40:5).

Playing shower games is a small price to pay to witness a wonder.

 ## Wacky Wives' Wisdom:

If you get blue or pink shower gifts, it will help determine the sex of the baby.

(What does lavender determine?)

No Way Out

I can do everything through him who gives me strength.
—*Philippians 4:13*

Sooner or later, we all come to this point in our pregnancy. It usually happens in the middle of the night or when you've had one of those days when your hairdryer, coffee maker, car, computer, and husband won't cooperate. It's the point when you realize: *There is no way out.*

Like all good panic, it starts small and builds, usually in direct relation to your girth. Somehow, the bigger the baby grows the more you wonder exactly how this is all going to work. When you seek the comfort of your spouse, however, this is what happens. Or at least this is what happened to me:

"What's wrong?" Mark asks me. "Why are you breathing like you've run a marathon? And why do you look as if something is all my fault?"

"I'm going to have a baby," I declare, even though it's been obvious for months.

"I know, but what's the problem?"

"I'm going to have a baby and I'm not pleased with the whole idea."

"It's perfectly natural, honey. Women have been doing it since time began. It should be no big—"

I stop him with a look.

"Take it easy, honey," he says, retreating a step. "It can't be that bad. Indian women used to give birth while squatting in the forest and then come back to their family, presenting them with the tiny bundle."

"Are you suggesting . . .?"

"No, no," he wisely says. "All I'm saying is you have nothing to worry about."

That's not what I want him to say.

He tries again. "We have a great doctor, wonderful nurses—"

That's not what I want him to say.

"I'll be with you every moment."

That's not what I want him to say.

He scans my body language, trying to figure out what I want from him. Then his eyes clear and shine with understanding. "I'm sorry," he says.

The magic words! The panic ebbs; my body relaxes. It's odd how two words have the power to soothe—and make me feel strong again.

I am woman. I am strong. And I can handle anything. Even having a baby.

 ## Wacky Wives' Wisdom:

Eating clay while pregnant relieves nervous tension.
(*I prefer my clay with Cool Whip and a cherry.*)

Birthing 101

Are your hearts tender and sympathetic? Then make me truly happy by agreeing wholeheartedly with each other, loving one another, and working together with one heart and purpose.
—*Philippians 2:1-2 (NLT)*

There is such a thing as too much knowledge.

We took childbirth classes before the birth of our first child, and a refresher class three years later before #2. But by #3, we didn't bother; we figured we had it down pat.

In every case, birthing classes were a mixed blessing. The fact that every facet of the birth has a title and a timetable (which each mother proceeds to amend and break with reckless abandon) was nonetheless reassuring. This was not a fly-by-the-seat-of-your-pants happening. Having a baby was a carefully detailed event. It seemed that the whole birthing process would be a very controlled experience.

I should have sued for false advertising.

Still, I was eager to learn it all—although that "transition" stage scared the living daylights out of me. Watching a movie of a birth was okay, too, as long as I was free to close my eyes during certain parts. (I figured it was good practice for closing my eyes during the real thing.)

Mark was not as eager. He was still hung up on those women throughout the ages (remember the Indian in the forest?) who had gotten along very well without the benefit of classes, videos, and birthing rooms. I informed him that if he expected women to ignore the advances of technology in regard to birthing babies, he would have to forgo the use of Novocain, TV remotes, and riding lawn mowers. He wisely acquiesced to progress.

He also observed that he "graduated" knowing more than he ever wanted to know about the biological process. In a way, I agreed with him. Both of us tend to be the type who accept the miracles of electricity, fax machines, and aspirin without the need to know exactly how they work. Same with birthing.

But whether we thought the classes yielded too much knowledge or not enough, they had a secondary—or perhaps a primary—purpose: they brought Mark and me closer together. They made us a team. They made us a family long before our two became more. Our graduation from *that* lesson was well worth the schooling.

Wacky Wives' Wisdom:

Let Mother Nature take her course.
　　(*Does that mean she's had a birthing course, too?*)

Sympathy Gains

If one part suffers, every part suffers with it; if one part is
honored, every part rejoices with it.
—*1 Corinthians 12:26*

You've heard of sympathy pains? My husband experienced sympathy *gain*. As I gained weight with my pregnancies, so did he. If I was eating for two, apparently he was eating for three. I appreciated the thought but told him it wasn't really necessary to try and match my waistline, inch for inch.

"No problem," he said.

"But there might be a problem," I said. "I get to lose a lot of this weight in a single shot. You don't have that advantage."

Good point. His weight leveled off soon after.

It has to be hard being the father-to-be. We mothers-to-be get the attention. We get the baby showers. We get to feel the baby's movement from the inside out. He experiences the pregnancy secondhand. So how do we make him feel more a part of the program? Give these a try:

1. Every time you wake up in the middle of the night to go to the bathroom, make him stumble through the dark with you.
2. Make him sacrifice the foods you've had to sacrifice: no caffeine, no artificial sweeteners, low fat. No double cheeseburgers with fries. Lots of milk, vegetables, and other edibles that have the audacity to contain vitamins.
3. Strap a few telephone books to his middle and have him negotiate the stairs, get in and out of the car, get up from the couch, sleep on his side, and tie his shoes.
4. Let him go to the doctor and be forced to lose all sense of modesty.
5. In the middle of the night, kick him in the ribs just like Baby kicks you.
6. Have him live with the idea of birthing a watermelon.

We *can* be nasty, can't we? Perhaps we should add one last one: Give him lots of love, sympathy, and foot rubs.

Sure, we could be totally wicked in our willingness to let our husbands experience pregnancy. But we won't, because we love them for making us mothers.

Wacky Wives' Wisdom:

Being pregnant makes you bald.
(Aren't our sympathetic husbands glad this one isn't true?)

Optional Equipment

"Therefore I tell you, do not worry about your life, what you will eat; or about your body, what you will wear. Life is more than food, and the body more than clothes."
—*Luke 12:22-23*

And baby makes three . . . thousand dollars.

Well, maybe the baby gear doesn't cost that much—but a second mortgage is an option. It's amazing that such a tiny being can require such a huge amount of equipment. I had visions of packing up Baby to visit Grandma with the same amount of baggage as a royal tour.

It starts with the baby's diaper bag, a.k.a. the Sanity Survival Kit. Inside we stash stuff to keep our baby, and therefore us, in a noncrying mode.

The meal equipment is complex. There are bottles made of glass, plastic, and rubber. Some are bent like elbows, and some have holes right through their middles. There are beginner cups, tippy cups, intermediate cups, and I-don't-need-it cups. There are silver spoons, plastic spoons, and even spoons that curve at a right angle, presumably so the target is more easily hit. And of course, there are the infamous baby wipes, used for both types of cheeks.

For the traveling family, there are battery-operated bottle warmers, car seats worthy of a tiny heir to a very wealthy throne, portable high chairs, booster seats, changing pads, cribs, and even portable potties. There are pull-down shades so the little darlings don't get the sun in their eyes. There are toys that hang from their car seat so they are never bored (are we setting a dangerous precedent here?).

Speaking of entertainment, there are tapes for baby to listen to, mobiles that play music, dolls that giggle, and other dolls that sound like a heartbeat so the baby won't even realize it's been born yet. There are toys made in blah black and white because some know-it-all determined that a newborn can't see color. (How do they know that? I know from personal experience that all of my children could recognize color immediately. How else could they appreciate their Chartreuse Caboose room?)

I haven't even touched on the nursery furniture. The crib with matching sheets, bumper pads, crib skirt, pillow, curtains, valances, wallpaper borders, changing-table covers, decals, mobiles, soft sculptures for the walls, stuffed animals, and even switchplate covers. They've got us, ladies. They know we like things to be coordinated; we have an it-must-match fetish. And we buy it. All of it. You've got to wonder what happened to sticking the baby in a drawer with Daddy's socks.

There are even intercoms that reinforce the fact that you and this baby will be joined at the hip for many, many years. Too long . . . and yet not long enough?

They grow up fast. They lift their heads, roll over, sit, and walk before you can pay off the equipment you bought to help them along the way. It's best to realize that the equipment is icing. The only equipment babies really need is a mother and father to love them—and that doesn't cost a thing.

Wacky Wives' Wisdom:

All babies are born with blue eyes.
(Uh-uh. I ordered green to match the walls.)

If Sarah Could Wait Ninety Years...

Wait for the Lord; be strong and take heart and wait for
the Lord.
—*Psalm 27:14*

Getting a little restless in your state of waiting? I know the feeling. I'm an impatient person. If there are more than two people ahead of me in the checkout line, I'm ready to take my business elsewhere. If they must have commercials on TV, then it is my responsibility to make wise use of the time by writing a letter or stirring the spaghetti sauce. If my daughter's concert is supposed to start at 8:00, I don't want it starting at 8:01.

It sounds like I'm a Type A personality, but actually, I'm a Type E—stuck in a rut of Efficiency. Time is precious to me, and I'm most happy when I'm able to use it wisely. The phrase "go for two" has special meaning in my life philosophy: don't do one thing at a time when you can do two. Or more.

Waiting for Carson's birth, I sewed thirty-one pieces of clothing for myself. It was a case of a delusional pregnant woman creating outfits to wear in her post-pregnancy based on her prepregnancy size. After Carson's birth, the "elasticity" of my waist resembled the elastic in an old pair of pajamas. Since it did not immediately snap back to its prebaby measurement, some of my new wardrobe had to be given to charity. Waist not, want not.

Oh, well. It kept me busy, which is the point and the cure for waiting. Keep moving. Don't sit around counting the minutes or interpreting every kick and twinge as the start of labor (believe me, you'll know it when it comes). Take heart in the fact that as a pregnant lady at least you know *it will come*. Think of those mothers-in-waiting who are trying to adopt. They don't just suffer through *when*, but often *if*.

Address the birth announcements, match up your husband's socks, alphabetize your spices, read Sarah's story in the Bible (if she could wait ninety years to get pregnant, you can wait a few more weeks to give birth). Or best yet, write the baby a letter telling how much you're looking forward to meeting him or her.

I guarantee your child is looking forward to meeting you, too. God's gifts are worth the wait.

Wacky Wives' Wisdom:

Crossing your legs creates varicose veins.
    (*Good. I was looking for an excuse to put my feet up.*)

PART 4

Pulling It Off

Show Time

For you created my inmost being; you knit me together
in my mother's womb.
—*Psalm 139:13*

You would think that with a second baby we would know the signs. . . .
As I got dressed in the labor room of the hospital to go back home after experiencing false labor, I started to cry.

The nurse put her arm around me. "There, there. What's wrong?"

"You must think I'm stupid," I said. "I've been here three times and gone home three times."

"We don't keep count," she said.

I nodded, hoping it was true. "I just want to have this baby!"

That's the crux of it. Our bodies are huge, our hormones are raging, the grandmas are in the starting gate ready to pounce, the camera has film, and the baby seat is in the car, ready for that first trip home. But your body won't cooperate.

With first babies, the problem lies in the fact that you have no idea what labor feels like. I remember sitting at my kitchen table with my sister-in-law Deanna and telling her, "I'm in labor." The veteran of two children, she shook her head. "If you were in labor you couldn't talk to me like this." Two days later, I proved her right.

But with the second baby, you would think I would recognize real labor when I saw it. No way. Remember my three false alarms? By the time the real labor started, we were so thrilled, we commemorated the moment by backing into Grandma's car.

For Laurel, there was another kind of timing issue. We were scheduled to go to London eleven days after her due date. I really needed her to be born on time. The day before the due date, I worked myself into quite a tizzy, trying to will myself into labor. I prayed, I used positive thinking, and, most of all, I begged. And then my mother remembered that she had used castor oil to induce one labor. If it's not time, it won't work, but if it is . . .

Apparently it was time, because eight hours after taking the awful stuff, I went to the hospital.

Each story was different and yet the same. In each case, there were those silent moments in the car on the way to the hospital when both Mark and I realized that within a short time our lives would be changed forever.

It gave us pause. It made us scared. Yet it made us strong. It was time.

Ready or not, the baby was coming.

 ## Wacky Wives' Wisdom:

Castor oil can induce labor.
(Sure; it tastes so bad the baby wants to abandon ship.)

Riding the Roller Coaster

"Come to me, all you who are weary and burdened, and I will give you rest."
—*Matthew 11:28*

Open your eyes! Look at your focal point!"

I opened one eye and managed to melt the speaker to silence. Somewhere in the back of my brain I knew I was forgetting everything I'd learned in the childbirth classes, but I didn't care. I didn't care about anything except getting through the pain. The pain was a roller coaster that grabbed hold of me and pushed me way too high before hurling me off the top. I've never liked roller coasters.

My eyes snapped open as I experienced a moment of calm, a break in the ride. *Oh, yes, this is what "normal" feels like.* . . .

My breath was sucked to my toes as I began another loop of the ride. My eyes clamped shut in anticipation of the drop-off. *Will it ever end?*

"Hang in there," Mark said as he pushed against my lower back—the epicenter of my pain.

How can I hang in there when I'm not wearing a seatbelt?

My mind drifted to thoughts of amusement parks. I would be taking a bite of a funnel cake drowning in cherries and powdered sugar when someone would grab me and toss me on that roller coaster again—

People came and went but I ignored them. They were outside my world. They were not in the car with me, but somewhere on the ground. They were safe. Waving at me, calling my name—

"Nancy? We're taking you to the delivery room. It won't be long now."

Sure, that's what they all say. Don't they know this ride doesn't have an end?

"Hop over on the other bed," they told me.

I emerged from my daze long enough to give another scathing look. Hop? I managed to slide from one roller-coaster car to the other. The sun had come out. It was bright and very warm.

Then suddenly, I wanted to go faster. Push, push this car. Faster, faster.

"Don't push yet," a woman said at my feet. "Hold on. Blow. Blow." I blew and blew, trying to apply the brakes.

"Now!" came the voice. "Push! Push!"

With utter relief I pushed. The forces of nature took control.

"Watch!" Mark said into my ear. "Open your eyes and watch!"

I shook my head. I was too busy. Besides, there was something else that overshadowed me, myself, and I: a new life. A soul was being born.

The force whooshed through my body. The soul left me. Separate now, we each took a breath. I heard a cry. Was it me?

"It's a girl!" Mark said. "It's a girl!"

I could open my eyes. I had reached the end of one ride—and was beginning another. This ride I would share with one who had been part of me for nine months and now was out on her own.

I held out my arms and drew her close.

"Hello, little one," I said.

It was time to meet the miracle.

 ## Wacky Wives' Wisdom:

You have to slap a newborn on the rump to get her to take her first breath.

(A slap doesn't do it. God does.)

Memory Block

"A woman giving birth to a child has pain because her time has come; but when her baby is born she forgets the anguish because of her joy that a child is born into the world."
—*John 16:21*

There's a song that goes, "Memories, pressed between the pages of my mind . . ." After the births of my children, two pages must have stuck together. The memories of the actual birth experience begin to fade before the hospital serves its first dish of lemon Jell-O. If it weren't so, the world would soon face a precipitous population drop.

Once I was settled in a hospital room, after both mother and child were clean and presentable, there was no thought of pain or struggle. The antidote was the feel of the baby in my arms. The infant's dependence on me pushed aside all thoughts of discomfort. I was finally *being a mother*.

Oh, I was still willing to rehash each detail of the progression of labor to whomever was willing (or even not willing) to listen. Yet the uniqueness of the baby was first and foremost on our minds: Emily's long fingers, Carson's pursed lips, Laurel's plentiful dark hair. And by the time we went home (*home:* the word took on new meaning), the sharp edges of the memories were already softening.

After Emily was born and some months had passed, it was Mark who brought up the subject of having another child. The first time he did so, I socked him in the arm. But as Emily grew into a toddler, that old yearning to hold a child—a child who didn't want to run away after ten seconds—resurfaced. I longed for the sweet smell of a baby's breath instead of the scent of peanut butter and jelly. I ached to have a baby's fingers wrap around mine instead of tug at me with an insistent, "Here, Mommy, here!"

So when Mark once again offered the question, "Wouldn't you like to have another baby?" I didn't sock him. This time, as Emily pulled all the magazines off the coffee table and proceeded to tear the covers off, I snuggled under Mark's arm and said, "Why not?"

Gullible fool? Masochist? Or loving mother? Perhaps they are one and the same.

Funny, I don't remember.

Wacky Wives' Wisdom:

Your IQ drops when you're pregnant.
   (*And doesn't increase until the kids leave for college.*)

Queen for a Day

Know that the Lord is God. It is he who made us, and
we are his; we are his people, the sheep of his pasture.
Enter his gates with thanksgiving and his courts with
praise; give thanks to him and praise his name.
—*Psalm 100:3-4*

You've heard all the stories about "drive-thru deliveries," hospitals discharging moms and babies just hours after birth. As the veteran of three births, my advice to you is to do everything in your power to resist this trend.

By the time Laurel was born, a hospital stay of less than twenty-four hours was standard. They had the gall to tell me, "You'll rest much better at home."

Excuse me? I had a seven-year-old and a four-year-old at home. In the hospital, I had a private room—something I hadn't experienced since my single days. I was *not* going home yet. So I pulled out all the stops. I cried. I got to stay. (There are times when common sense does prevail.)

I loved being in the hospital. Giving birth was the only time in my life I was admitted for a positive experience. It was a celebration. My hours were filled with visitors bearing gifts and flowers. I enjoyed a dinner with Mark, uninterrupted by children arguing over who gets the biggest brownie. When the phone rang it was not someone trying to clean my carpets, have me change long-distance carriers, or participate in a survey, but a well-wisher offering words of congratulations. I didn't have to cook, clean, or even get dressed. My only task was to enjoy my baby and wallow in the joy of it all.

I could handle this.

For a little while I was special. I was a queen sitting in her bedchamber, accepting the accolades of her subjects. Reality would set in soon enough.

And I would handle that, too.

Wacky Wives' Wisdom:

Don't take flash pictures of your newborn. It can damage her eyes.

(And please, don't take any *photos of a woman who has just emerged from hours and hours of labor.)*

Mine!

He chose to give us birth through the word of truth, that
we might be a kind of firstfruits of all he created.
—*James 1:18*

My baby.
   What a song those words sing!

I was very quick to take possession of my daughters and my son. *Gimme, gimme! They're mine!*

I can't say I felt much like sharing. Just as I would have to teach my children the virtues of not hoarding their possessions, I had to learn not to hoard *them*. Daddy deserved a turn. Grandmas, grandpas, cousins, and aunts. All wanted to sing the wonderful song, if only for a time: "My baby!"

Sharing was made even harder by the fact that I could easily justify my selfishness. After all, wasn't it I who had just given up nine months of my normal life in order to nurture this child into existence? If you reap what you sow, as Jesus tells us, I had sown the seed to harvest. Or, consider the words of Moses: "He will love you and bless you and increase your numbers. He will bless the fruit of your womb, the crops of your land" (Deut. 7:13). Wasn't it natural I should get first dibs?

Not exactly.

For, while Mark and I may have *conceived* the child, the *gift* of the child originated Somewhere else: "Every good and perfect gift is from above, coming down from the Father of the heavenly lights, who does not change like shifting shadows" (James 1:17). My baby was God's baby first.

My babies were on loan. They were mine to cuddle, coddle, and cherish; to drive, discipline, and defend; to grieve over, glory in, and grumble about. Yet one day far too soon, they will venture out on their own to find a life independent of mine. I will have to stand in the doorway with my feet aching to run after them. I will have to wave and smile as if my heart wasn't breaking to see them go. I will have to close the door, yet keep it handily unlocked so they can return if they need me. For they will need me, just as I need them. And though I will have told them about God, it will be up to their hearts and their minds to accept him or reject him. I can only pray. . . .

But that's the future. I accept it as part of the package of motherhood. For now, the baby is mine. My baby. Thank God.

Wacky Wives' Wisdom:

You lose a tooth for every child.
(But you never lose a child, not completely, not ever.)

Look Who's *Here*

May your father and mother be glad; may she who gave
you birth rejoice!
—*Proverbs 23:25*

It was two in the morning. I stood in front of the nursery door and peeked into the room. Mark came up behind me and whispered in my ear, "What are you doing?"

I put a finger to my lips, shut the door without a sound, and pulled him down the hall. "Shh, she's sleeping."

"Exactly," he said. "When she's sleeping you're supposed to sleep."

"I can't."

"Why?"

"Because she's *here*."

"And she's going to be *here* for at least another eighteen years," he said. "There's a good chance you're going to need sleep before that."

"I don't mean that kind of 'here,'" I explained. "I mean, she's *here*. She's *alive*."

Mark shook his head. "In that case, you're going to have to add another sixty or seventy years onto your scenario. That's a long time to stand at the door and—"

"I worry."

"You shouldn't. She's healthy. Happy. *Sleeping*. Which is what we should—"

I shook my head. I knew he was right. Logical. Sensible. But I didn't want to be any of those things.

Mark turned me around, put his hands on my shoulders, and marched me toward the bedroom. Just as I was beginning to protest, we were stopped in our tracks by a sound. "Whaa . . . mmm . . . ekwhee. Mnab." Our daughter was awake.

He gave me a dirty look. "You rigged that so you could go see her. You *willed* her to wake up."

I hadn't, but I filed away the idea for the future. I moved toward the nursery door.

"I'm going to bed," he said as the baby's sounds grew louder. Then he stopped in the doorway of our room. "Nancy?"

I turned toward him, my face beaming with the anticipation of spending more time with our child.

"I'm glad she's *here*, too."

 ## Wacky Wives' Wisdom:

You shouldn't baby a baby or she'll grow dependent on you.
    (*That's exactly what I had in mind.*)

The Mother's Oath

So we fix our eyes not on what is seen, but on what is
unseen. For what is seen is temporary, but what is unseen
is eternal.
—*2 Corinthians 4:18*

Now that your baby is born, it is time to take the Mother's Oath. Raise your
right hand and repeat after me:

I hereby apologize—in advance—for every time I will complain about my children. I solemnly promise to praise them lavishly, love them outlandishly, and protect them prudishly. I will do my best to fulfill my duty as teacher, guide, cookie maker, and chauffeur.

I will expect perfection only as far as *I* am perfect. I will grab hold when I'm needed, stand to their side when appropriate, and fling them loose when they need a push.

I will show them all the world has to offer and teach them to relish the good and abhor the bad. I will show them by example how the bad can be made better through the good works of good people.

I will teach my children about God. I will not preach. I will strive to have God's love shine through my words and actions so that my children cannot help but see the wonder of his presence. They will want what he and I are oh-so-willing to share.

They will see that Me, Myself, and I is an unholy trinity. They will learn to give graciously of their time, talents, and treasures.

I will help my children recognize their gifts; urge them to find their purpose; and encourage them to merge their will with God's will for their lives.

I will show them how to give thanks in all things. I will let them make mistakes and remind them that through struggle we gain strength.

My children will know with every breath of their being that I like them. I cherish them. And I love them.

They can count on me until the day I die. So help me God.

Welcome to motherhood.
Good luck, and may God be with you!

About the Author

Nancy Moser is the author of *Motherhood: A Celebration of Blessings &Blunders*, as well as several other books of inspirational humor and a series of Christian novels. She has three perfect children and a very tolerant husband.